wordsworth
GRASMERE

'The loveliest spot that man hath ever found'

In association with Scala Arts and Heritage Publishers Ltd

'Perfect Contentment, unity entire'

'A Whole without dependence or defect,
Made for itself, and happy in itself,
Perfect Contentment, Unity entire'

Home at Grasmere, 1800

WILLIAM WORDSWORTH WROTE these lines at Dove Cottage, Grasmere, in 1800, shortly after returning to his beloved Lake District with his sister Dorothy. Today, Wordsworth Grasmere is home to one of the finest literary house museums in the world, visited by tens of thousands of people each year. A visit here is a unique experience; nowhere else does so much of a major writer's original work remain where it was written and inspired.

At Wordsworth Grasmere we celebrate poetry, people and place. Through the words of William and Dorothy – in luminous poetry and prose – we bring to life a revolutionary moment in English literary history. We tell the story of the extraordinary people who lived here, and we celebrate the stunning Lake District landscape that inspired them – now a World Heritage Site.

William told a friend that through his poetry, he aimed 'to console the afflicted, to add sunshine to daylight by making the happy happier, to teach the young and the gracious of every age, to see, to think and feel'. He calls for us to reconnect with nature, asks that we show empathy for others, and encourages us to nurture our creative imagination.

A visit to Wordsworth Grasmere, in the footsteps of William and Dorothy, is both a step back in time and a recognition that the greatest poetry is timeless in its meaning and relevance.

Michael McGregor
Director

'There is a small house at Grasmere empty'

IN NOVEMBER 1799, while on a walking tour with his brother John and the poet Samuel Taylor Coleridge, William noticed a cottage for let. Built in about 1700, in the late eighteenth century the cottage had been licensed as an alehouse called The Dove. It stood directly on what was then the main road through the central Lake District, passed by regular traffic of waggons, carriages and people on foot or horseback. In 1805 Dorothy commented 'the cottage was on the highway of the tourists'.

The Wordsworths did not know their home as Dove Cottage – this name was first recorded in a census in 1851. To them, the address was Town End, Grasmere. They moved in on 20 December 1799, initially for an annual rent of £5. Funded by a private income, the Wordsworths lived here for eight years. Their neighbours, the Ashburners and the Fishers, helped them make their 'little domestic slip of mountain' into a Garden-Orchard (see p. 24).

As the family grew, the Wordsworths moved across the valley to the larger, newly built house of Allan Bank in May 1808.

Circle of James Bourne (1773–1854), *Dove Cottage and Helm Crag*, grey wash, about 1800

'What happy fortune were it here to live!'

For William and Dorothy Wordsworth, moving into Dove Cottage in 1799 was a homecoming in the fullest sense: as a boy, William had glimpsed Grasmere from Loughrigg, the fell at the south end of the lake, and exclaimed, 'What happy fortune were it here to live!'

Now, after a decade of unsettled wandering, he was back in the Lakes – where he was born – and above all, he was with his beloved sister, Dorothy. Orphaned as young children and separated for years, the two had lived together recently in other people's houses, through the generosity of friends. Now they could make a home together.

Dorothy's absorbing journal is a detailed record of joint labours in the house and garden. William's poem 'Home at Grasmere' is an expression of utmost gratitude for life in this place and with Dorothy, whose voice, he says, 'was like a hidden bird that sang'. The household radiated welcome – to Mary Hutchinson, who married William in 1802, to Mary's sister Sara, to mariner-brother John Wordsworth, to the poet Samuel Taylor Coleridge. And soon to William and Mary's children as well.

'Where'er my footsteps turn'd,
Her Voice was like a hidden Bird that sang;
[continues top of page illustrated]
The thought of her was like a flash of light
Or an unseen companionship, a breath
Or fragrance independent of the wind;
In all my goings, in the new and old
Of all my meditations, and in this
Favorite of all, in this the most of all.'

William Wordsworth, *Home at Grasmere*, written out by Dorothy in 1806

'There was a time…'

MAKING A HOME IN Grasmere nourished William as a poet. His depiction of the Lake District and its communities, what he was later to call 'the Republic of Shepherds', made up much of the enlarged second edition of *Lyrical Ballads* of 1800. Here too he embarked on his greatest work, *The Prelude*. The finest of William's meditative poems, the 'Ode: Intimations of Immortality', belongs to the Dove Cottage period. It was conceived as he was digging dung into the vegetable garden, a true coming together of life and art.

William Wordsworth's poems continue to speak to us because they are grounded in the fundamentals of life – joy in the natural world and physical sensation (as in his best-loved poem, 'I wandered lonely as a Cloud'), love of parent and child (found in 'Michael', the story of a Grasmere shepherding family), and grief. His elegy for his brother, John, drowned in a shipwreck, is a lament that all readers can share, as are the heartfelt musings on the loss of youthful vision in the 'Intimations' ode. And long and demanding though it is, *The Prelude*, William's sustained examination of his own life in its historical setting, will still engage all readers who have ever attempted to understand the development of their own lives.

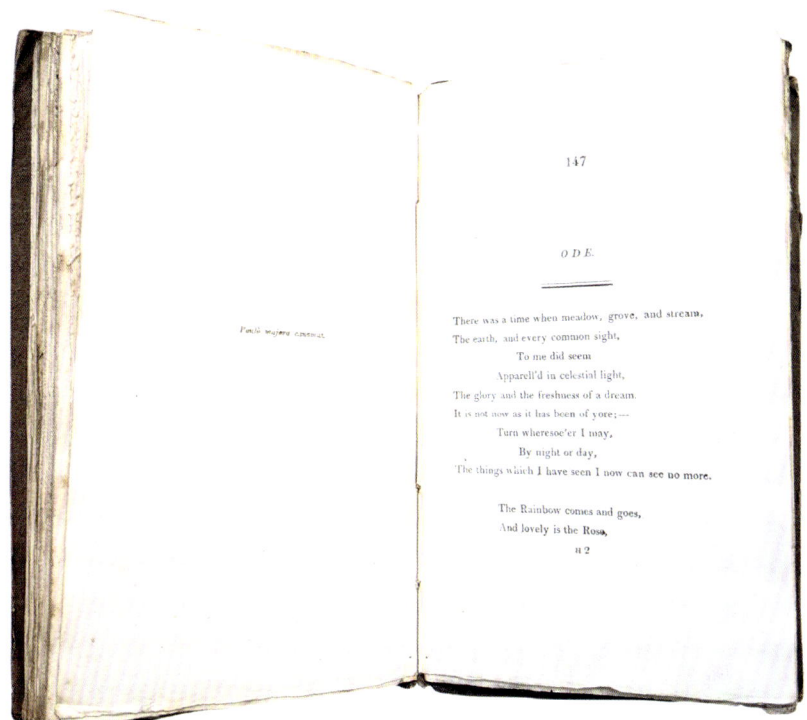

William Wordsworth, 'Ode', as first published in *Poems, in Two Volumes*, 1807

'I resolved to write a journal'

DOROTHY WORDSWORTH LONG dreamed of a settled life with her favourite brother, William. When only six years old, and shortly after her mother's death in March 1778, Dorothy left her Cumbrian home to spend her childhood with relatives in Halifax. From 1788 until settling with William in Dorset in 1795, she moved between family and friends. In Dorset Dorothy and William met Coleridge, beginning a remarkable friendship that saw them move to Somerset to be closer to him. Finally, settling with William at Dove Cottage in 1799, her dream came true: 'An object long desired, we had returned to our native mountains'.

Dorothy wrote hundreds of letters throughout her life, keeping family and friends close and in touch. When William went away for three weeks in 1800 she began a journal as a way of continuing conversation with her absent brother. She continued the journal until January 1803, by which time William was married.

For the reader, the journal brings the Wordsworths' day-to-day existence to life. Dorothy records everything, from the reading and writing of poetry to the smallest domestic details and the daily activities of walking and gardening. She carefully records her and William's exchanges with people they met on the road and visitors to the cottage. The journal also includes multiple examples of what Coleridge described as 'Her eye watchful in minutest observation of nature'.

As well as letters and journals, Dorothy wrote out thousands of lines of William's poetry as part of the cycle of drafting, fair copying and revising his work. Although modest about her own abilities, Dorothy was certainly a poet in her own right. She wrote about thirty poems altogether, five of them by 1808.

'The small birds are singing – Lambs bleating, Cuckow calling – The Thrush sings by Fits, Thomas Ashburner's axe is going quietly (without passion) in the orchard'.

Dorothy Wordsworth, Grasmere journal, 6 May 1802

Dorothy Wordsworth, Grasmere journal, showing the passage quoted

'Do go, dear Rain! Do go away!'

William, Dorothy and poet Samuel Taylor Coleridge spent a remarkable year together in Somerset from 1797, which resulted in their collaborative book of revolutionary poetry, *Lyrical Ballads*. A few months after the Wordsworths settled at Dove Cottage, Coleridge sought to continue their friendship by moving with his family to Greta Hall in Keswick, 13 miles north of Grasmere. The two families were frequent overnight lodgers in each others' homes, with Coleridge spending lengthy periods at Dove Cottage. On one visit he lay in bed listening to incessant rain, composing a poem ,'Ode to Rain', which ended:

> 'But only now, for this one day,
> Do go, dear Rain! Do go away!'

Coleridge was energised by the mountains, exploring them alone and on foot, and without a map. On one nine day 'circumcursion' of the highest fells he descended Broad Stand on Scafell, England's second-highest mountain, hanging from and dropping down a series of ledges one by one. In August 1800 he extended the journey from Keswick to Grasmere by taking a detour via Helvellyn, England's third-highest mountain. He ended his 21-mile walk at Dove Cottage late at night, as Dorothy records in her journal: : 'At 11 o'clock Coleridge came … We sate & chatted till ½ past three W in his dressing gown. Coleridge read us a part of Christabel'.

However, the Wordsworths were deeply anxious about Coleridge's health, which was badly affected by his heavy intake of opium. His unhappiness was increased by his frustration at what he saw as his lack of success as a poet, and his unrequited love for Sara Hutchinson, William's sister-in-law. These feelings inspired one of his greatest poems, 'Dejection: An Ode', published on 4 October 1802 – the same day that William and Mary Hutchinson were married.

Coleridge left the Lakes in 1804 in search of better health in the warmer climes of the Mediterranean. He took with him specially prepared manuscript versions of William's then unpublished poems, including newly composed parts of the 'Poem to Coleridge', which we now know as *The Prelude*. Coleridge treasured these pages, his 'companions in Italy', keeping them safe despite, as he tells us, returning in 1806 'shirtless and almost penniless. My manuscripts, excepting two pocket notebooks, either in the sea or taken back to Malta'.

George Dance (1741–1825), portrait of Samuel Taylor Coleridge, pencil, 1804.

'we had returned to our native mountains, there to live'

DURING THEIR FIRST YEAR in Grasmere, William and Dorothy were joined by their younger brother John. 'We are daily more delighted with Grasmere, and its neighbourhood' wrote Dorothy, nine months after arriving. That autumn, John left the household to take up his duties as Captain of an East India Company ship.

Over time, William and Dorothy's affinity and familiarity with the valley and its community grew. They named many local places after family, weaving themselves into the landscape. In John's Grove, a small wood near Dove Cottage they named after their brother, William and Dorothy lay on the ground: 'William heard me breathing & rustling now & then but we both lay still, & unseen by one another' wrote Dorothy in her journal.

William credited Dorothy with teaching him observation and sensitivity:

'She gave me eyes, she gave me ears;
And humble cares, and delicate fears;'

'the lonely roads were schools to me'

WHILE WALKING, WILLIAM and Dorothy frequently encountered people who would often inform and inspire their writing. Dorothy recorded such encounters in her journal: 'we met an old man almost double ... his trade was to gather leeches but now leeches are scarce & he had not strength for it...'.

William took the character of the 'leech-gatherer' as the subject for his poem 'Resolution and Independence'. The narrator of the poem describes listening to the old man talk, and sees strength in him as a character:

'And soon with this he other matter blended,
Cheerfully uttered, with demeanour kind,
But stately in the main; and, when he ended,
I could have laughed myself to scorn to find
In that decrepit Man so firm a mind. "God,"
said I, "be my help and stay secure; I'll think
of the Leech-gatherer on the lonely moor!"

James Burrell Smith (1822–1897), *Approach to Grasmere*, pencil, watercolour and bodycolour, 1846

'we have made it neat and comfortable within doors'

Dorothy's letters written at Dove Cottage include detailed descriptions of the family home: 'Our house is literally and truly a cottage … a little low-roofed Building, with its entrance through the kitchen' … '[It's] quite large enough for us though very small, and we have made it neat and comfortable within doors'. 'We have… a small orchard and a smaller garden which as it is the work of our own hands we regard with pride and partiality'.

In March 1802 Dorothy describes the composition of a poem set in their garden:

Dorothy Wordsworth, letter to Lady Beaumont, 26 August 1805, in which she describes Dove Cottage to her friend

'William had slept badly … while we were at breakfast… he, with his Basin of Broth before him untouched… he wrote the Poem to a Butterfly! He ate not a morsel, nor put on his stockings but sate with his shirt neck unbuttoned, & his waistcoat open while he did it. The thought first came upon him as we were talking about the pleasure we both always feel at the sight of a Butterfly … I wrote it down & the other poems & I read them all over to him… he began to try to alter the butterfly, & tired himself.'

'We are crammed in our little nest edge-full'

WILLIAM AND DOROTHY were not living in isolation. Neighbours and friends visited the cottage, and their friend and fellow poet Coleridge was a frequent guest (page 7). There would be many other notable visitors, including a young admirer, Thomas De Quincey, who would live here as a writer after the Wordsworths left (page 37). Mary Hutchinson, a childhood friend, married William in 1802. Dove Cottage was their first family home.

Sadly, within a year, news would reach Dove Cottage of their brother, John, who had died tragically at sea:

> 'The meek, the brave, the good was gone;
> He who had been our living John
> Was nothing but a name.'
>
> William Wordsworth, 'Elegiac Verses', 1806

'We are crammed in our little nest edge-full … Every bed lodges two persons at present', wrote Dorothy in March 1806, a year that saw the arrival of William and Mary's third child.

Yet it was in this crowded home that William's great poetry was written, an achievement remarked on by his sister just prior to their move to Allan Bank: 'I cannot but admire the fortitude, and wonder at the success with which he has laboured, in that one room, common to all the Family, to all visitors, and where the children frequently play beside him.'

William at work among his family. A scene taken from the Wordsworth Grasmere introductory film

'We sate by the kitchen fire'

THE KITCHEN WAS the domestic centre of the house – a place of comings and goings, with cooking, but also sewing and mending, ironing and eating. Here the siblings would read, pen letters and Dorothy would write in her journal. They kept their door open to passing strangers, offering them a little money or food and listening to their stories. The fireplace seen here today is a later addition – that of the Wordsworths's time being much larger.

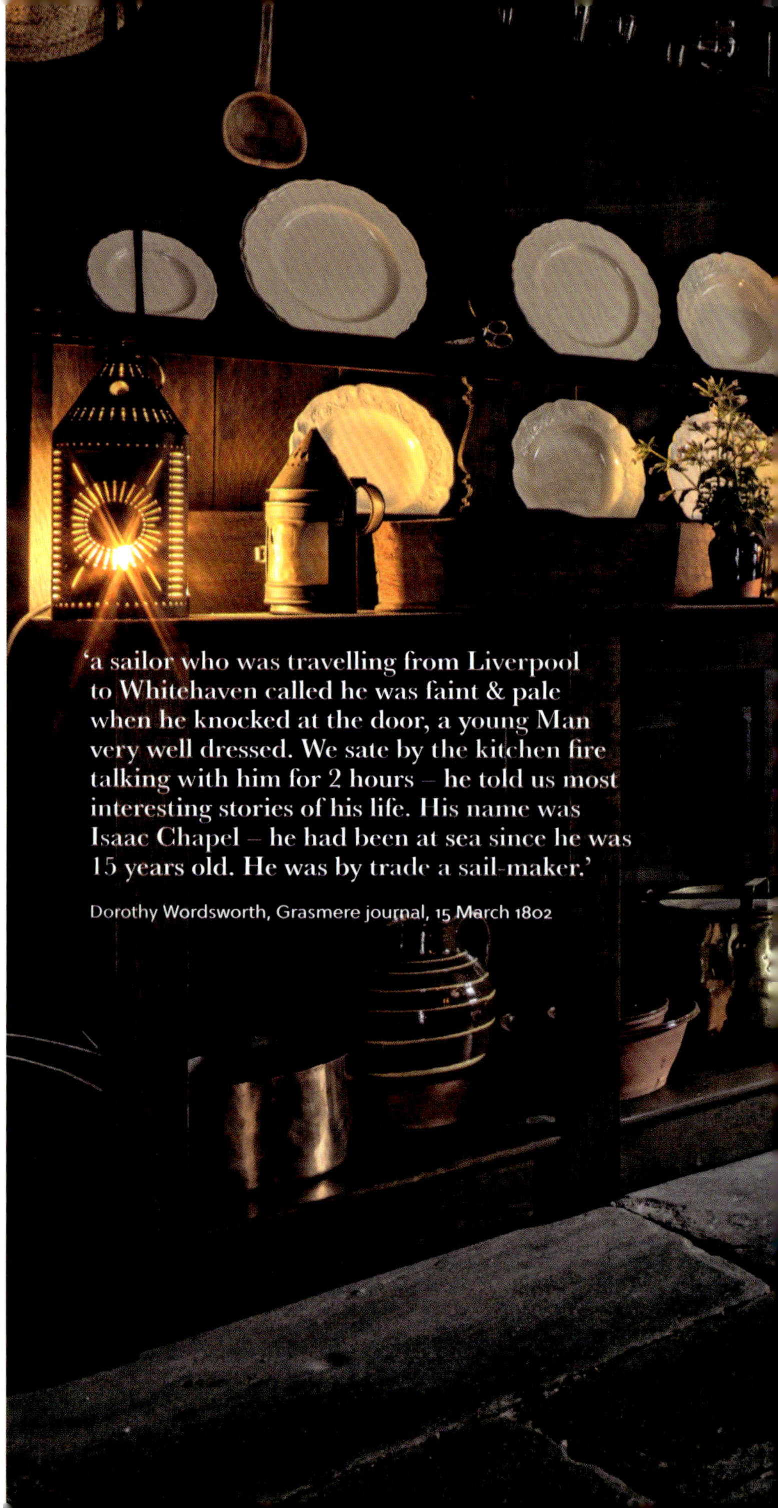

'a sailor who was travelling from Liverpool to Whitehaven called he was faint & pale when he knocked at the door, a young Man very well dressed. We sate by the kitchen fire talking with him for 2 hours – he told us most interesting stories of his life. His name was Isaac Chapel – he had been at sea since he was 15 years old. He was by trade a sail-maker.'

Dorothy Wordsworth, Grasmere journal, 15 March 1802

'We have made a lodging room of the parlour'

THIS ADJACENT DOWNSTAIRS room was used as a lodging room, or bedroom, first by Dorothy and then, by mid-June 1802, by William. It became William and Mary's room after their marriage in 1802, a room they shared with their children after the birth of their son John in summer 1803.

'We have made a lodging-room of the parlour below stairs, which has a stone floor therefore we have covered it all over with matting.'

Dorothy Wordsworth, letter to Jane Marshall,
10 and 12 September 1800

'He [Johnny] can sit upright on the carpet, and so we leave him – sometimes he gets a good bump upon his head and lustily he roars…'

Dorothy and William Wordsworth, letter to Samuel Taylor Coleridge, 6 March 1804

'D[ora]. is of the dancing brood, and given to ecstasy; but John is of a more sober and thoughtful nature. As to Thomas, he is grown a very stout healthy-faced child, and can almost walk alone…'

'I feel deeply every hour of my life the riches of the Blessing which God has given us, and you who have nursed your own Babe by a cottage fire-side know what peace and pleasure, wakefulness and hope there is in attending upon a healthy infant'.

Dorothy Wordsworth, two letters to Catherine Clarkson, 30 August 1807 (top) and 13 November 1803

'Baking bread apple pies, & a Giblet pie'

THE WORDSWORTHS NEVER refer to this room by name. It was probably used as a typical back kitchen or scullery; a place for washing and laundering of clothes, baking and cooking. The Wordsworths employed several people to help out during their time here, most notably Molly Fisher, a woman of about 60 in 1800, who lived in the cottage opposite, and who helped 'light the fires wash dishes &c &c'.

NEXT TO THE BACK kitchen is a small, naturally cold room, with water rising between the floor slates after rain. Dorothy mentions not wishing to disturb William's sleep by fetching more fuel for the fire on a cold night – this may suggest that this room was used as a peat store. It may also have been a cold store for food.

'[Molly] has washed all the linen of all our visitors except the Family of the Coleridges during [July]. I help to iron at the great washes about once in 5 weeks, and she washes towels stockings, waistcoats petticoats, &c once a week such as do not require much ironing'

Dorothy Wordsworth, letter to Jane Marshall, 10 and 12 September 1800

'Baking bread apple pies, & Giblet pie – a bad giblet pie – it was a most beautiful morning.'

Dorothy Wordsworth, Grasmere journal, 3 July 1802

'Plain living and high thinking'

THE SITTING ROOM upstairs is the nearest William had to a study, albeit it with 'the children frequently play[ing] beside him'. It was also a place for breakfast, card-playing and collecting 'about the tea table', an occasion that could be 'prolonged into a meal of leisure and conversation'. On different occasions it was used as a bedroom by Dorothy and by Coleridge.

A young admirer of William's, Thomas De Quincey, later published his recollections of a visit to Dove Cottage in 1807:

> 'There was, however, in a small recess, a library of perhaps three hundred volumes, which seemed to consecrate the room as the poet's study and composing room; and such occasionally it was. But far oftener he both studied, as I found, and composed on the high road … The two or three hundred volumes of Wordsworth occupied a little, homely painted bookcase … They were ill bound, or not bound at all – in boards, sometimes in tatters; many were imperfect as to the number of volumes … in short, everything showed that the books were for use, and not for show'

'Miss Wordsworth I found making breakfast in the little sitting-room. No urn was there; no glittering breakfast service; a kettle boiled upon the fire, and everything was in harmony with these unpretending arrangements … This, thought I to myself, is, indeed, in his own words, "Plain living, and high thinking"'

Thomas De Quincey, recollections of a visit in 1807

'I have been literally at work from morning till night … We have been engaged, Mary and I, in making a complete copy of William's Poems for Poor Coleridge to be his companions in Italy … There are about eight thousand lines.'

Dorothy Wordsworth, letter to Catherine Clarkson, 25 March 1804

'William was disturbed in the night by the rain coming into his room'

THE UPSTAIRS ROOM adjacent to the sitting room was always used as a bedroom, with brothers William and John sharing it in 1800 until the latter's departure that September. From then until they swapped rooms by June 1802, William slept here, with Dorothy occupying the room below. It became the children's bedroom and a lodging room for guests, on at least one occasion both at the same time.

'The moon shone upon the water below Silver-how, & above it hung, combining with Silver how on one side, a Bowl-shaped moon the curve downwards – the white field, glittering Roof of Thomas Ashburner's house, the dark yew tree, the white field – gay & beautiful. Wm lay with his curtains open so that he might see it.'

Dorothy Wordsworth, Grasmere journal, 12 December 1801

'I was awakened by a little voice'

'That night I found myself, about eleven at night, in a pretty bedroom … Early in the morning I was awakened by a little voice, issuing from a little cottage bed in an opposite corner, solilo-quizing in a low tone. I soon recognised the words, "Suffered under Pontius Pilate; was crucified, dead, and buried;" and the voice I easily conjectured to be that of the eldest amongst [Wordsworth's] children, a son, and at that time about three years old.'

Thomas De Quincey, extract from his recollections of a visit in 1807

'My room is in the outjutting...'

As with the back kitchen below this room, the Wordsworths make little mention of a 'lumber room' other than reference to 'a sort of lumber room' in 1800, and in a letter of 1805 in which Dorothy describes the layout of the cottage: 'My Room is in the outjutting ... and there in the same part is also the pantry, Lumber room &c.'

> 'a Box of clothes with Books came from London. I sate by [William's] bedside, & read in the Pleasures of Hope to him, which came in the Box'
>
> Dorothy Wordsworth, Grasmere journal,
> 1 February 1802

'I have papered with newspapers'

DOROTHY DESCRIBED THIS room in 1800 as 'a small low unceiled room, which I have papered with newspapers and in which we have put a small bed without curtains'. Five years later it was improved and became her bedroom.

> 'We have got the roof of the peat room raised but the walls are new plaistered and it will be the end of summer before it is fit to be slept in'.
>
> Dorothy Wordsworth, letter to Catherine Clarkson, 8 June 1805

'Sweet garden-orchard, eminently fair'

'LET NATURE BE ALL IN ALL', so decreed William when it came to gardens. William and Dorothy desired to have predominantly native wild flowers growing in their garden – rather than the fashionable exotics being introduced into the country – unique for its time. Dorothy collected many of these wild plants from around the cottage: 'I rambled on the hill above the house gathered wild thyme & took roots of wild Columbine'. For its size, the garden contains an exceptional variety of plants: mosses, ferns and wild flowers.

Significantly, William and Dorothy's attitudes were in keeping with evolving changes in art and literature, examining how nature was to be viewed and interpreted; the latter became the cornerstone of the Romantic movement, in which William played such a pivotal role.

William summed up their love of the garden in his poem 'Farewell':

> 'Sweet garden-orchard, eminently fair
> The loveliest spot that man hath ever found'

This garden was not just a lovely space, it was inspirational. The plants and animals contained within the garden frequently feature in William and Dorothy's writings, with Dorothy making extensive comments on the garden and its plants in the journals she kept while living at Dove Cottage: 'Speedwell, that beautiful blue one the colour of the blue-stone or glass used in jewellery'.

A truly historic space, Dove Cottage garden not only contains tangible physical features of the past, but also conjures up events brought alive in the poetry and prose of William and Dorothy.

'Let Nature be your Teacher'

GARDENS ARE EVER-CHANGING. Since William and Dorothy tended the garden, generations of gardeners have left their own mark in the features and plants contained in it. Therefore the garden can never be the same as it was in the Wordworths' day. But very helpfully, William made it clear as to how a garden should be looked after: 'The rule is simple… work, where you can, in the spirit of nature, with an invisible hand of art.' This attitude endures today, with plantings of the wildflowers that they loved and an informality inspired by nature. It is a garden very much in the spirit, if not the letter, of their own.

In 1804 the Wordsworths created a 'moss hut' at the top of their garden-orchard at Dove Cottage. It was to be a space for contemplation, conversation and creativity:

> 'We have lately built in our little rocky orchard a little circular Hut lined with moss like a wren's nest, and coated on the outside with heath…'

> '… a place for my Brother to retire to for quietness on warm days in winter for a pleasure-house, a little parlour for all of us in the summer – it is large enough for a large party to drink tea in'.

William Wordsworth, letter to Sir George Beaumont (above), and Dorothy Wordsworth, letter to Lady Beaumont, both Christmas Day 1804

'The Rainbow comes and goes,
And lovely is the Rose…'

'after dinner William added a step to the orchard steps'

Dorothy Wordsworth, Grasmere journal, 8 May 1802

In 2020 Charlie Whinney, Harriet Fraser and Rob Fraser reimagined the Wordsworths' hut for the present day. During the Covid lockdown Charlie created the hut using sustainable Cumbrian oak: the spirals represent William and Dorothy; the holes and frames reveal meditative views. Visitors are welcome to spend time in the reimagined hut in the Sensory Garden: enter and sit awhile.

'Do again excuse my villainous pen, paper, and ink …'

THE WORDSWORTH GRASMERE MUSEUM displays some of the greatest treasures in English literature, accompanied by multimedia displays with responses by people living today. It is worth taking a moment to think about the manuscripts and books on display, each created by hand. The paper used in the early years was handmade from pulped linen rags – rags were scarce, paper was expensive. Folded sheets were handstitched into homemade notebooks, while full or part sheets were used for letter-writing.

Once written, the letter was folded to make a small packet for an envelope called an 'entire', which would be held in place with a wax seal. The recipient usually paid the postage, and this could be expensive, depending on the number of pages and the distance the letter had travelled.

People wrote with feather quills (usually from a goose or swan) with pointed ends that quickly blunted. The ink was homemade from a recipe of oak galls, iron sulphate and gum arabic.

It is worth thinking too of what these letters and books meant to those who owned them. Letters could bring news of the everyday, but also of births and deaths, and changes of fortune. Or they might contain words to be treasured, as in the case of William's letter to Mary in 1810, which she said was 'the first letter of love that has been exclusively my own – Wonder not then that I have been so affected by it'.

'Poems ... to be considered as experiments'

William Wordsworth and Samuel Taylor Coleridge, *Lyrical Ballads, with a Few Other Poems*, 1798

TO READERS OF HIS OWN time, William Wordsworth's poetry appeared strikingly new in its verse forms, language and choice of subject matter. William, Dorothy and Coleridge spent a remarkable year together (1797–98) in Somerset, from which came a new poetry for a new age published in *Lyrical Ballads*. These poems were a radical experiment, thought by many to have revolutionised English literature. The first poem is Coleridge's 'Rime of the Ancyent Marinere'.

In the volume's prefatory 'Advertisement' William criticises the gaudy and inane poetical language fashionable at the time. Instead, he seeks to prove the suitability of 'the language of conversation in the middle and lower classes of society' for poetic use. He expands this claim for his poems' experimental nature to include their subject matter, chosen from 'low and rustic life'. William writes about the homeless, about beggars, shepherds and people with disabilities, showing the essential humanity of these marginalised members of society. The poet claims that such people display 'the essential passions of the heart'. Through these choices of language and subject matter, William strives to make poetry more democratic.

'We have all of us one human heart!'

In April 1800 Coleridge visited Dove Cottage and work began on a new edition of *Lyrical Ballads*, this time with a second volume. Coleridge and his family moved permanently to Keswick later that summer.

The second edition of *Lyrical Ballads* had several important additions: it identified Wordsworth as its author on the title page and included poems on subjects that associated him with the Lake District. A new 'Preface' explored a definition of poetry, further developed in 1802 as 'the spontaneous overflow of powerful feelings: it takes its origin from emotion recollected in tranquillity'.

In his poem 'The Old Cumberland Beggar', William writes lines that are central to his belief in a shared humanity and our basic need to be kind to others. In 1835 he stated that if his poems are to continue to please, it will be 'for the single cause, "That we have all of us one human heart!"'.

William Wordsworth, lines towards 'The Old Cumberland Beggar', 1799

'I never saw daffodils so beautiful'

THE FOUR NOTEBOOKS that make up Dorothy's Grasmere journal are on display in the galleries. One of these, written in 1802, describes the joy that she and William shared at the surprise of seeing 'a long belt' of daffodils 'about the breadth of a country turnpike road' along the shores of Ullswater. Capturing this moment in her journal, Dorothy describes how the daffodils 'tossed & reeled & danced' in the wind.

Dorothy's prose is a record of shared pleasure in the beauty and energy of the natural world. Her sentences have a meticulous, eye-on-the-object immediacy; but they are carefully crafted – building details gradually and culminating in an evocation of spontaneous unlimited delight.

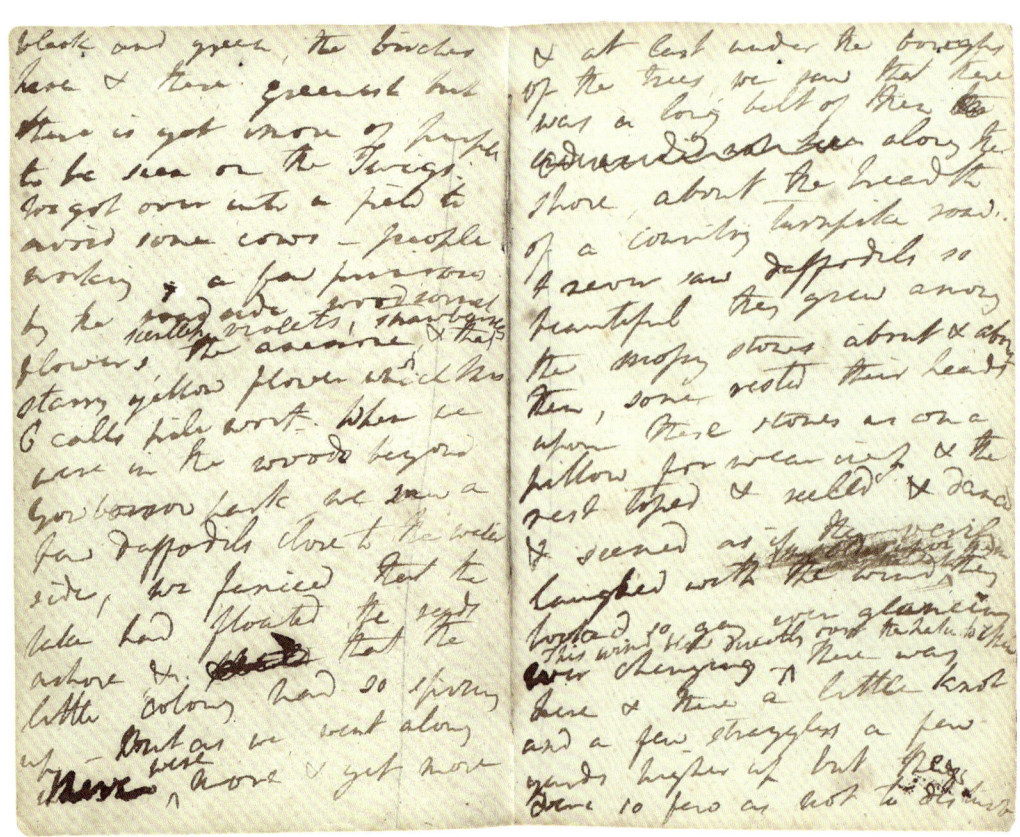

Dorothy Wordsworth, Grasmere journal, 15 April 1802

'I wandered lonely as a Cloud'

TWO YEARS LATER, in 1804, when William wrote a lyric poem describing a 'host of golden daffodils', he perhaps recalled that particular walk and Dorothy's prose – but his poem celebrates a solitary encounter and visionary joy. When first published, 'I wandered lonely as a Cloud' consisted of three six-line stanzas. An additional verse between the first and second stanzas was added when the poem was republished in 1815.

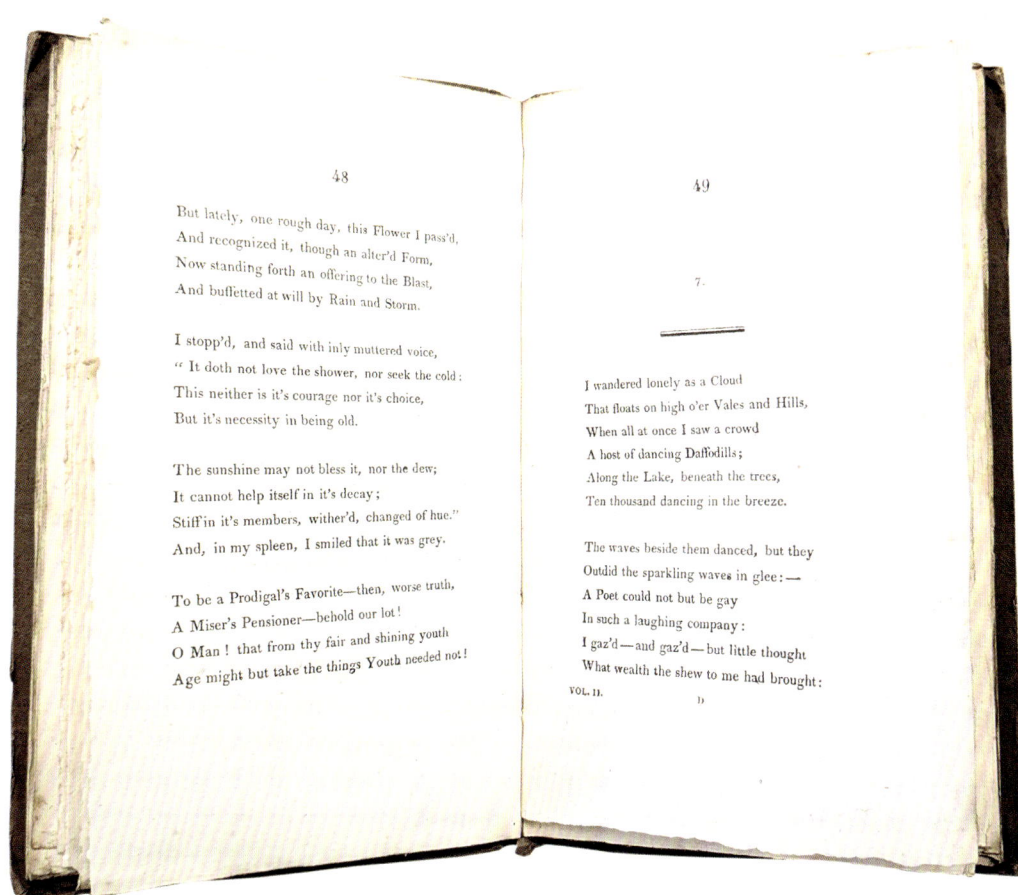

William Wordsworth, 'I Wandered Lonely as a Cloud', as first published in *Poems, in Two Volumes*, 1807

The Prelude
'The growth of a poet's mind'

THE PRELUDE IS A LITERARY masterpiece, the first major autobiographical poem in English. The Wordsworth Museum's *Prelude* gallery tells the story of the poem's long and complex creation and of the collaborative nature of its production. Known throughout William's lifetime as 'The Poem to Coleridge', the poem owed a great deal to Dorothy and Mary for their dedicated work of copying and recopying different versions over four decades.

William initially completed a two-part version in 1799, when he was 29 years old. He developed the poem into a 13-part epic of 8,487 lines by 1805, repeatedly returning to work on it throughout the rest of his life. It was not until 1850, just after his death, that *The Prelude* was first published and given its title.

To the poet, *The Prelude* was the 'poem on the growth of my own mind', begun as an exploration of the experiences that made him a poet.

Mary Wordsworth, 'An inmate of the heart'

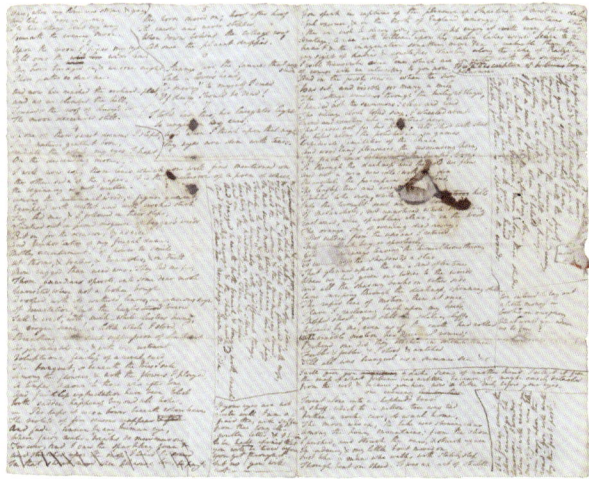

WILLIAM PAYS TRIBUTE to his wife, Mary, in *The Prelude*, describing her as 'an inmate of the heart'. Like Dorothy, Mary was central to the production of *The Prelude*. Over five decades she wrote out fair copies of the full poem as it then existed in 1799, 1804, 1805 and 1832. This amounts to over 20,000 lines of poetry written out with a quill pen.

Margaret Gillies (1803–1887), portraits of William and Mary Wordsworth, watercolour on ivory, 1839

In this extraordinary letter William sends his new poetry about his childhood to Coleridge. Dorothy has written out the poetry, which includes boyhood 'spots of time' – skating on Windermere and 'stealing' a boat at night. These would become key episodes in *The Prelude*. She is limited by the size of the paper, cramming in words where she can.

William and Dorothy Wordsworth, letter to Coleridge, 14 or 21 December 1798

Our greatest treasure is the earliest surviving version of *The Prelude*, in 13 books. Dorothy wrote out this version, sometimes with William reading the 'old copy' aloud. Although paper was expensive, she used only one side of each leaf, leaving the other blank for William's alterations. Some of these alterations were made at this time, others added ten or more years later.

William Wordsworth, *The Prelude*, written out by Dorothy Wordsworth, 1805 and 1806

Thomas De Quincey 'one of the family'

THOMAS DE QUINCEY, one of the greatest British prose writers, lived in Dove Cottage from 1809 until 1820 and continued to rent it for another 15 years, during which time he used it principally to store his books.

Born in Manchester in 1785, De Quincey was a brilliantly gifted boy who, at around the age of 14, read a manuscript copy of William Wordsworth's poem 'We Are Seven'. Inspired, De Quincey wrote a fan letter to Wordsworth in 1803, but it was another four years before he found the courage to accept the poet's invitation to visit him at Dove Cottage. Soon, wrote Dorothy Wordsworth, De Quincey seemed 'one of the Family'.

When the Wordsworths moved out of Dove Cottage in 1808, De Quincey moved in. Although his relationship with them flourished, De Quincey was keeping a secret: since 1804 he had been tampering with opium, and when Wordsworth's daughter Catherine died suddenly in 1812, De Quincey's grief pushed him from recreational use into habitual abuse. He recounted this time in *Confessions of an English Opium-Eater* (1821), widely considered the first modern drug memoir.

De Quincey met Margaret Simpson, the daughter of a Lakeland farmer, around 1813. Three years later she gave birth to their first child, William, and in 1817 they were married in Grasmere church. The Wordsworths disapproved.

The newlyweds and their baby retreated to Dove Cottage, where De Quincey's opium addiction began to produce vivid dreams: 'I was standing … at the door of my own cottage', he recalls in *Confessions*. 'Right before me lay the very scene which could really be commanded from that situation, but exalted, as was usual, and solemnized by the power of dreams'.

In 1820 De Quincey moved his family to nearby Fox Ghyll, and then eventually to Edinburgh, but it was not until 1835 that he gave up the rental on Dove Cottage. This was a painful decision: De Quincey wrote in 1840 that Dove Cottage had been 'endeared … to my heart so unspeakably beyond all other houses, that even now I rarely dream through four nights running, that I do not find myself (and others beside) in some one of those rooms'.

Sir John Watson Gordon (1788–1864), portrait of Thomas De Quincey, 1845

A 'little huckster's shop' (1862)

THOMAS DE QUINCEY'S 26-year tenancy of Dove Cottage saw many changes, inside and out: 'rooms new papered – kitchen underdrawn – and many other comforts', wrote Dorothy in 1808. Bookshelves were made by the Grasmere joiner and the sitting room came to resemble a study. Hedges were removed in the garden, much to the dismay of the Wordsworths!

Mrs Letitia Luff, a friend from the Wordsworths' Dove Cottage days, lived here in the late 1830s; Mrs Cookson and daughters, family friends once living in Kendal, resided here from 1843 while their new home of Howfoot, nearby in Town End, was being completed.

The first recorded naming of 'Dove Cottage' in a census comes in 1851, when a coal agent, Christopher Newby, and his family resided here. Sometime after 1850 a new first floor was added to the adjoining outbuilding of the cottage.

John and Jane Dixon ran the cottage as a 'lodging house' and shop in the 1860s, with a visitor mentioning 'a little huckster's shop' in what had been the Wordsworths' sitting room. Mrs Agnes Yeoman ran a lodging house in 1871 (living with five other adults and four young daughters), and Wilson Cole and John Armstrong and their families welcomed boarders through the 1880s.

Thomas Ogle (probably), earliest-known photograph of Dove Cottage

The Dove Cottage Trust (1891)

EDMUND LEE, AN ADMIRER of Dorothy Wordsworth, bought the house in 1888, letting it to the last private tenant, Charles Walmsley – who had named his daughter Dorothy Wordsworth Walmsley.

Dove Cottage first opened to visitors on 27 July 1891, following a fundraising appeal led by the Rev. Stopford Brooke, a devoted Wordsworth scholar and one-time chaplain to Queen Victoria. The Wordsworth Trust (originally called The Dove Cottage Trust) was set up five months later, with Stopford Brooke as its Chairman. Other founding trustees included Prof. William Knight, another important early Wordsworth scholar, and Canon Hardwicke Rawnsley, who went on to co-found the National Trust.

Postcard of Dove Cottage from the early 1890s. Notice the absence of a porch, and sash window frames rather than the current small diamond panes in lead cames (changed in the 1890s)

A 'Designated Collection' (1997)

STOPFORD BROOKE'S VISION included 'a low-roofed, simple museum, shaded by trees; the little cottage beside it'. The Wordsworth Trust quickly received donations of furniture, possessions, books and paintings with Wordsworthian connections. However, the collection was transformed in 1935, when a major archive, containing William's verse drafts, Dorothy's journals, correspondence and other important papers, was received by bequest from Gordon Graham Wordsworth, the poet's grandson. It is this archive that makes Dove Cottage unique: nowhere else in Western literature can so much of a major writer's original work be seen where it was both written and largely inspired.

The bequest was made 'on condition that a few of the more interesting features of the Collection … be displayed'. A museum was created in the barn next to Old Sykeside in 1935, and in 1981 it was moved to its current location, a former hotel coach house beside Dove Cottage: Stopford Brooke's vision had been realised.

In 1997 the collection's 'national and international importance' was recognised through the Government's Designation scheme. It was one of the first museum collections in the country to be given this status. In 2005 the Wordsworth Trust created the Jerwood Centre, giving the collection a new purpose-built home. Its research facilities are used by people from all over the world.

In 2020, to mark the 250th anniversary of Wordsworth's birth, Dove Cottage was reimagined with new interpretation, the Museum was expanded, the Learning Space was created and the Sensory Garden and the Woodland were opened. The whole experience was renamed 'Wordsworth Grasmere'.